Grade 1

Enrichment Reading

T5-ACR-303

Challenging and Fun Activities
Critical Thinking • Problem Solving
Creative Thinking • Comprehension

Table of Contents

Table of Contents (continued)

Credits:
McGraw-Hill Consumer Products Editorial/Production Team
Vincent F. Douglas, B.S. and M. Ed.
Tracy R. Paulus
Jennifer Blashkiw Pawley

Design Studio
Cover: Beachcomber Studio
Interior: Color Associates

Warner Bros. Worldwide Publishing Editorial/Production Team
Michael Harkavy   Charles Carney
Paula Allen   Allen Helbig
Victoria Selover   Holly Schroeder

Illustrators
Cover & Interior: Animated Arts!™

McGraw-Hill
Consumer Products
A Division of The **McGraw·Hill** Companies

Send all inquiries to:
McGraw-Hill Consumer Products
250 Old Wilson Bridge Road
Worthington, Ohio 43085

1-57768-291-2

2 3 4 5 6 7 8 9 10 QPD 04 03 02 01 00 99

LANGUAGE ACTIVITY

Bingo

Ask some of your friends to play this game with you.

Make a grid similar to the one below for each player.

Players should write each word below in one box of the grid. The words can be in any order.

Have one of your friends read the words in random order, one at a time. The players should circle each word on their paper as the word is said.

The person who circles three words in a row should call out "Bingo!"

Continue playing until all the words have been called out.

jump	likes	to
cage	and	read
go	see	tiny

Problem Solving Activity

Go Home

Use your finger to trace a path through the maze to connect the dog to the puppy. Then use a blue crayon to mark the path. Use a different colored crayon to connect each of the other animals to its friend.

Can you help (Runt) go to the (puppy)?

Can you help (Buttons) go to (Mindy)?

Can you help (Squit) go to the (baby bird)?

4

What Can You See?

Think about what you might see in a birdcage, a refrigerator, a fish tank, and out of a window. Draw a picture to illustrate each scene.

100%

SCIENCE ACTIVITY

Where Do I Live?

Look at the animal pictures at the bottom of the page. Draw a line from the animal to the box showing where it lives. Think about other animals that are found in each setting. Circle the animals that could be pets.

6

CRITICAL THINKING ACTIVITY

What Can You Ride?

Here is an activity that you can do with a friend.

Put an X on the things that you can ride on land. Draw a line under the things you can ride on water. Circle the things that you can ride in the air.

On another sheet of paper, draw other things that you can ride.

7

MATHEMATICS ACTIVITY

Find the Pets

Find and count the dogs, cats, birds, and fish in the picture. Write the numbers on the lines.

 7   dogs   8   cats

6   birds   5   fish

CRITICAL THINKING ACTIVITY

What Is In It?

Identify each object on the left and decide which object in the row would most logically be inside. Circle your choices.

9

Make a Pet Robot

Here is an activity for you to do with a friend.

You will need to gather the following materials: large and small cereal boxes, craft sticks, pipe cleaners, bottle caps, buttons, beads, paste, and colored markers.

Once you have finished creating your pet robots, tell each other stories about your pets.

LANGUAGE ACTIVITY

My Dog

Unscramble the words in each group to make a sentence. The first word in each sentence is in the right place. Write each sentence on the lines.

1. I big dogs like.

   I like big dogs.

2. My is dog big.

   My dog is big.

3. My swim can't dog.

   My swim can't dog.

4. I dog park to the walk my.

   I walk my dog to the park.

11

MATHEMATICS ACTIVITY

Time Out!

Look at the sample clock and digital watch at the top of the page. The long hand on the clock shows the minutes and the short hand shows the hour. Show the time when you do each activity on the clock and write the time on the digital watch.

I get up at this time.

I go to school at this time.

I go out to play at this time.

I eat dinner at this time.

I go to bed at this time.

LANGUAGE ACTIVITY

Shape Up!

Put the words listed below in the right shape. Look carefully at the shape of the letters to make sure they fit in the spaces.

Skippy   lesson   pencil
paper   squirrel grade

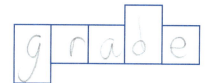

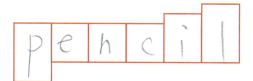

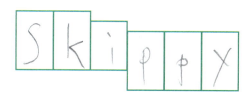

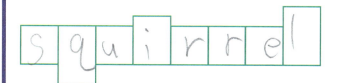

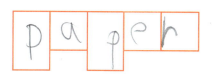

SOCIAL STUDIES ACTIVITY

May I?

Look at the pictures at the bottom of the page. Write the number of each picture next to the sentence that describes it.

You may do this in the water.	6	You may not do this in the water.	4
You may do this at the zoo.	1	You may not do this at the zoo.	3
You may ride like this.	7	You may not ride like this.	5
You may play here.	2	You may not play here.	8

1

2

3

4

5

6

7

8

14

Come Out and Play!

Think of a book you like to read. Who do you wish could come out and play with you? Draw a picture.

SOCIAL STUDIES ACTIVITY

Stop and Go

What color is **STOP**?   What color is **GO**?

Look at the first box. Look at the color of the light that is showing, then choose and circle the object in the box that is usually the same color as the light. Repeat this activity with the other boxes.

LANGUAGE ACTIVITY

Make A Word

Draw a line from a trailer to the back of each car to complete a word.

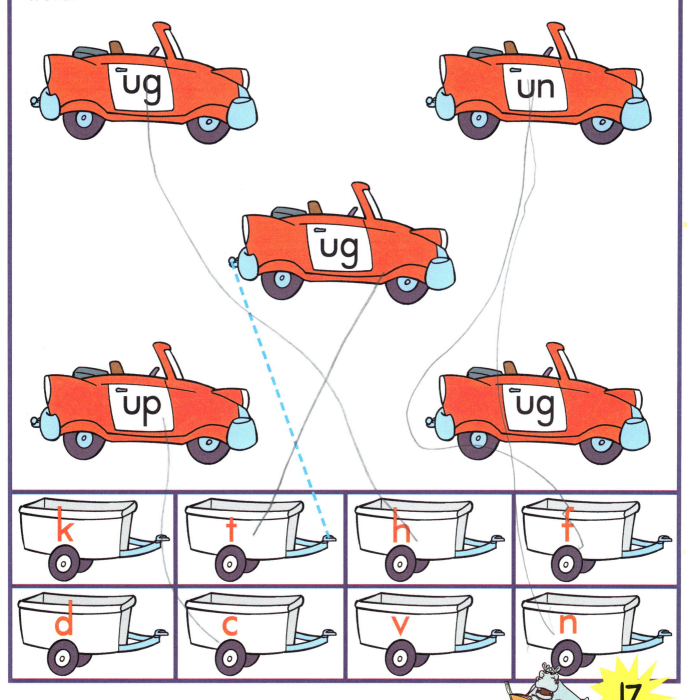

Sail Away!

You can make a boat!
Ask an adult to do this activity with you.
Find the following materials: an empty half-gallon
milk carton, a square of paper, a plastic straw, and a piece of clay.

1. Cut the milk carton in half,
or have an adult cut it for you.

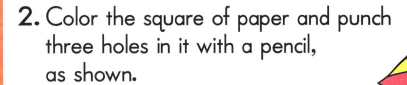

2. Color the square of paper and punch
three holes in it with a pencil,
as shown.

3. Run a straw through the paper
and stand the straw in the carton.
Hold it in place with a piece of clay.

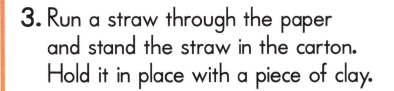
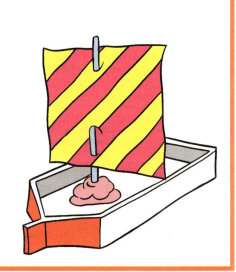

Set your boat afloat in a pond, pool, or tub.

LANGUAGE ACTIVITY

Moon Code

Each symbol used below stands for a letter. Use the code. Write the words. Then say the words.

1.

a	f	c	t

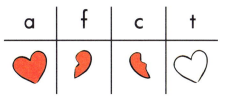

fat   cat

2.

w	t	e	p

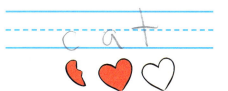

wet   pet

3.

m	e	u	o	J	n

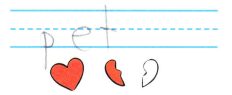

June   moon

CREATIVE THINKING ACTIVITY

Circle Fun

A circle can be a sun. What else can it be?
Draw a picture using each circle.

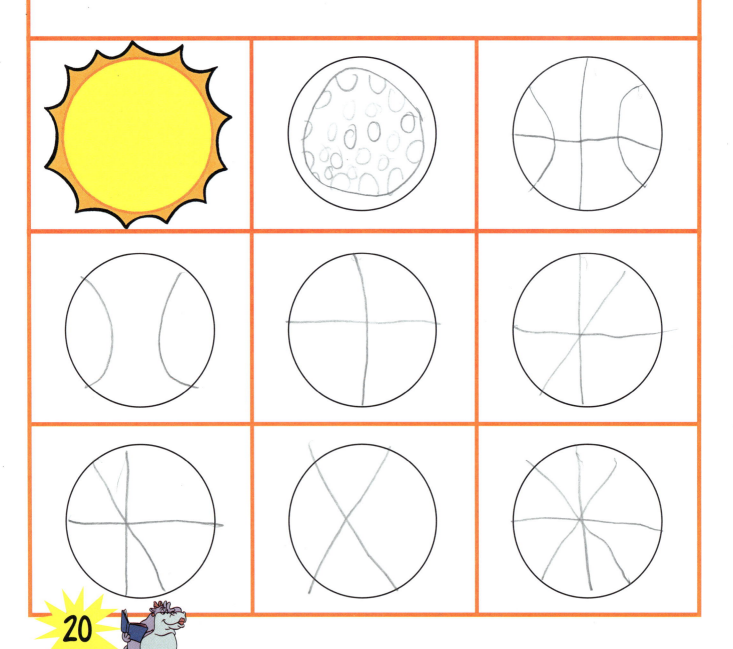

20

LANGUAGE ACTIVITY

What Is My Name?

Each letter of the alphabet has a symbol. Use the code to make names. Write the names.

A	B	C	D	E	F	G	H	I
○	□	△	☆	Ⱳ	⊞	⊙	◇	☺

J	K	L	M	N	O	P	Q	R
◰	⟞	▽	▭	✚	✕	⋈	◑	♡

S	T	U	V	W	X	Y	Z	
⊕	⊗	▣	▽	⊠	⊓	⇧	⇩	

Write your name in code.

SCIENCE ACTIVITY

Pictures in the Sky

Wakko likes to look at the stars at night.

If you look at the stars, you can see the pictures they make. These star pictures are called constellations.

Find the star pictures. Draw a line from the stars to the picture they make.

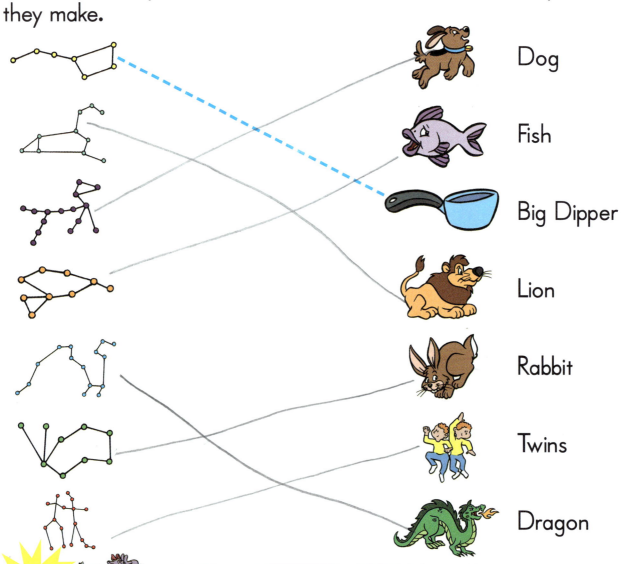

Dog

Fish

Big Dipper

Lion

Rabbit

Twins

Dragon

CRITICAL THINKING ACTIVITY

Pick A Pet

Draw a picture of your favorite pet. Then tell why you picked this pet. If you do not have a pet, pick one that you would like to have. Tell why you would like to have it.

My Favorite Pet

_____

_____

_____

_____

_____

_____

_____

MATHEMATICS ACTIVITY

In The Tank

Find out how many of each fish are in the tank.

Fill in one square for each fish you count.

Go Fish!

This is an activity for you to do with a friend. Together, you can discover what objects a magnet attracts.

Tie a piece of string to one end of a pencil or stick. Tie a small magnet to the other end. Collect small objects (metal and nonmetal), such as nails, chalk, paper clips, pennies, crayons, safety pins, and erasers. Place the objects in a fish bowl or tank and take turns "fishing." Score one point for each object "fished out" by the magnet.

PROBLEM SOLVING ACTIVITY

At The Beach

Read each sentence. Then draw a picture showing the scene described in each sentence.

1. Three shells are by the water.

2. Bits of wood are by the water.

3. A bird is in the sky.

4. A fish is jumping out of the water.

5. A little green boat is in the water.

Picture Frame Collage

Use shells to make a frame collage. If you can't find shells, use pasta shells! Other materials you will need are a square of cardboard, scissors, paint, glue, and tape.

Read the directions. Frame a photograph of yourself to give as a gift to a member of your family.

1. Draw a square in the middle of a piece of cardboard.

2. Cut out the square.

3. Paint the frame. Let it dry.

4. Glue shells on the frame.

5. Tape a picture on the back of your frame.

Finger Puppet Play

Do this activity with one or more friends. Make puppets! Put on a play!

Gather old gloves, scissors, markers, bits of felt, and glue. Read the directions.

Practice your parts and present a puppet play to your family and friends.

1. Cut the fingers off an old glove.

2. Draw on eyes, a nose, and a mouth.

3. Cut out bits of felt for ears, hair, and a tail. Glue them on.

4. Read your part. Put on a play for your class.

Duck Rabbit Runt Squit Slappy Skippy Rita

Social Studies Activity

Make Up Your Mind!

What do you like to do?

Put a check next to the thing you like to do best.

Sit down with a friend. Find out what your friend likes to do. Find out what things you both like to do.

1. Go to the aquarium ___ or go to the zoo ___

2. Swim in the water ___ or walk in the woods ___

3. Look for rocks ___ or look for shells ___

4. Ride on a pony ___ or ride in a boat ___

5. Jump like a frog ___ or hop like a rabbit ___

6. Pet a cat ___ or pet a dog ___

7. Read a book ___ or see a play ___

8. Feed a fish ___ or feed a bird ___

9. Play tag ___ or play ball ___

10. Ride a bus in the city ___ or ride a car in the country ___

Name That Tune!

Yakko likes to sing songs.
What songs do you like to sing?
Write the names of two songs you like.

Make a flute to hum your songs. Ask an adult to help you collect a cardboard tube, a pencil, a small square of waxed paper, and a rubber band. Follow the steps listed below to make a flute. Use the flute to hum your songs to a friend. Your friend should try to guess the song.

1. Put four holes in a tube. Use a pencil.

2. Put a piece of waxed paper over one end of the tube.

3. Put a rubber band over the paper to keep it in place.

4. Move your fingers over the holes and hum a song.

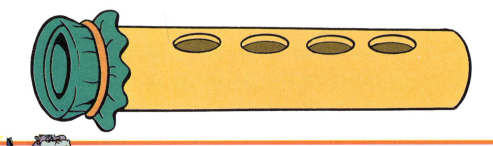

Print A Leaf

Slappy and Skippy like to trace leaves and draw. It is also fun to print leaves.

With a friend, collect the following materials: leaves, glue, cardboard, poster paint, paintbrushes, and drawing paper. Read the directions and follow the steps for making leaf prints.

Try to identify the leaves by looking for them in books.

1. Put glue all around the top of a leaf. The top is the smooth side.

2. Glue the leaf to a piece of cardboard.

3. Put a little paint all over the leaf.

4. Press the cardboard onto a piece of paper. Press hard.

5. Pick up the cardboard. You can print many leaves this way!

SOCIAL STUDIES ACTIVITY

New Things

Each year you do many new things. Read each sentence. Write your answer.

1. What new thing did you learn to do?

_____

2. What new place did you go to?

_____

3. What new thing did you get?

_____

4. What new book did you read?

_____

CREATIVE THINKING ACTIVITY

A Good Name

Elmyra's rabbit looked like a ball of snow. Snowball was a good name for her.

Think of a good name for each animal. Write the name on the line.

On a separate sheet of paper, draw one of the animals you named.

1. A turtle

_____

2. A mouse

_____

3. A cat

_____

4. A lion

_____

5. A frog

_____

6. A pony

_____

CRITICAL THINKING ACTIVITY

Did You Hear That?

Read each sentence. Think of when you might say each sentence. Write **winter**, **spring**, **summer**, or **fall** on the lines.

1. "It is fun to play outside in the snow."

   winter

2. "The red leaves are so pretty."

   fall

3. "It is too hot to play in the sun."

   summer

4. "Did you see the new green leaves?"

   spring

5. "It will be cold soon."

   winter

PROBLEM SOLVING ACTIVITY

Find A Word

Find each of the words in the puzzle and circle them. Words are written vertically and horizontally.

flower	tree	string	wolf	fish	nuts
blast	house	squirrel	hat	spring	gray

```
w   s   q   a   n   p   f   h   b   s
h   n   u   t   s   l   i   a   m   q
u   r   g   h   o   u   s   e   q   u
b   w   o   l   f   m   h   i   h   i
l   g   p   r   l   c   s   n   x   r
a   h   a   t   o   m   p   i   l   r
s   e   v   n   w   r   r   m   g   e
t   r   e   e   e   g   i   y   r   l
i   w   a   t   r   m   n   d   a   a
n   s   t   r   i   n   g   t   y   n
```

35

RESEARCH AND REPORTING ACTIVITY

Animal Book

Pick an animal to tell about. Make a book about the animal you pick. Look in a book. Try to find out these things.

1. What does it look like? _____

2. Where does it live? _____

3. How does it move? _____

4. What does it do during the day? _____

5. What does it do at night? _____

6. What does it eat? _____

7. What can it do that is special? _____

Write what you find out about your animal. Use as many pages as you need.

Make a cover for your book. Write the name of your animal and draw a picture. Then put all of the pages together.

Blowing In The Wind

Make a pinwheel and see it turn in the wind!

Gather the following materials: a square of paper, crayons, scissors, a thumbtack, and a pencil with an eraser. Follow the directions below.

1. Take a square piece of paper. Color both sides.

2. Draw two lines and a circle. See the picture.

3. Cut along each line up to the circle.

4. Fold four corners to the middle. See the pictures.

5. Put a thumbtack in the middle to hold all the ends.

6. Put the thumbtack into the eraser end of a pencil.

Now, hold on tight and be careful the wind's not too strong or you could end up flying to Holland.

CRITICAL THINKING ACTIVITY

Which Is It?

Your <u>kite</u> ought to be like your <u>face</u>—different from everybody else's. Don't you think? If you make a kite of your own, you could draw a big picture on it so you could see it when your kite was flying. If you and some friends were flying your kites together, you would know which kite was yours.

What about these kites? They all look the same, don't they? One kite is different. Look closely. Find the kite that is different. Then circle the two things that make it different.

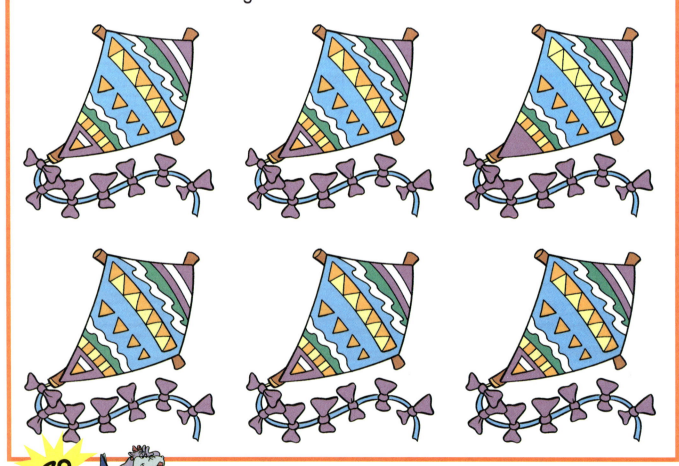

NAME _____

CRITICAL THINKING ACTIVITY

Sorting It Out

Look at the toys below. How are they alike?
Sort the toys by making groups for toys that are alike in some way.
Write your reasons on the lines below.

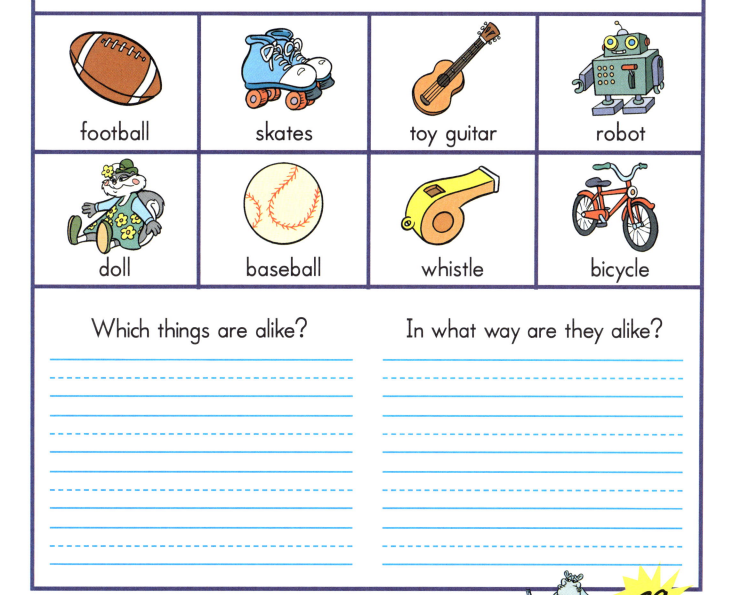

| football | skates | toy guitar | robot |
| doll | baseball | whistle | bicycle |

Which things are alike?

In what way are they alike?

_____

_____

_____

_____

_____

Busy Words

Many words mean more than one thing. Read each pair of sentences. Find the word below that can fit in both sentences. Write the word in each blank.

light	play	fly	watch
change	right	leaves	fall

1. a. My dog never does anything ___right___.

   b. I write with my _____ hand.

2. a. There is a _____ in my soup!

   b. The bird learned to _____.

(continued)

LANGUAGE ACTIVITY

Busy Words

3. a. Carlos turned on the _____ .

   b. The little dog is very _____ .

4. a. The _____ are on the ground.

   b. I don't like it when my grandmother _____ .

5. a. Yakko and Dot _____ in the park.

   b. Emily saw the _____ Snow White.

SCIENCE ACTIVITY

Can You Sense It?

Your five senses tell you things about every place you go. Think of a place you like. Close your eyes and imagine you are there.

Answer the questions about the things you can sense at the place.

What are three things you can see?

_____

- -

_____

What are three things you can hear?

_____

- -

_____

What are three things you can smell?

_____

- -

_____

What are three things you can taste?

_____

- -

_____

What are three things you can touch?

_____

- -

_____

CREATIVE THINKING ACTIVITY

How Many Ways?

Do this activity with one or more friends. Take turns naming words to describe each item on the list below.

How many ways can —

1. grass feel?

2. a burp sound?

3. a cat look?

4. the sky look?

5. a sneaker smell?

6. a pickle taste?

7. a voice sound?

8. a pillow feel?

43

LANGUAGE ACTIVITY

Time For A Rhyme

Yakko, Wakko, and Dot were "as snug as three bugs in a rug." The words *snug*, *bug*, and *rug* rhyme.

Look at the sentences below. Look at the list of words below and find the one that rhymes with the underlined words in each sentence. Write a rhyming word in the blank. Be sure the sentence makes sense.

took	word	mat	bed	night

1. The <u>cat</u> <u>sat</u> on the ___mat___ .

2. <u>Look</u> at the <u>book</u> I _____ .

3. The Brain has a <u>light</u> to <u>write</u> at _____ .

4. I thought I <u>heard</u> that <u>bird</u> say a _____ .

5. We <u>fed</u> baby <u>Ned</u> and put him to _____ .

44

Shapes To Feel

"Taking over the world requires a good sense of touch. Sometimes I have to touch Pinky sharply on the shoulder to make him think. But your friends are probably smarter.

Make a touching box with one of them. Make sure that you have the following: cardboard, scissors, scraps of velvet, sandpaper, sponge, satin, felt, plastic, corduroy and other materials, glue, and a shoe box.

One of you should read the directions for making the box. Be sure it's you."

1. Cut shapes out of cardboard. Make two of each shape.

2. Now cut shapes to match out of different things. You can use velvet, sandpaper, sponge, satin, felt, or plastic. Glue the shapes on the cardboard.

3. Glue one set of shapes to the top of a shoe box. Cut a hole in one end of the shoe box so that your hand can fit in. Put the other set of shapes in the box.

4. Put your hand in the box and feel one of the shapes. Tell which one you think it is. Then take it out and match it to the shape on the top of the box. If you are right, you get one point. Take turns and match all the shapes.

MATHEMATICS ACTIVITY

Food For Sale

Write **Yes** or **No.** Then tell how much change you will get or how much more you need.

 FISH 45¢

 PIZZA 50¢

 HOTDOG 25¢

 TACO 30¢

 APPLE 5¢

 BANANA 7¢

 ICE CREAM 10¢

 MILK 6¢

1. You have  Can you get an ice cream?

    Yes, 5¢

2. You have
    Can you get two milks?

3. You have
    Can you get a fish?

(continued)

Food For Sale

4. You have 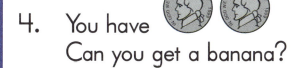 Can you get a banana?

_____

5. You have  Can you get pizza?

_____

6. You have  Can you get three apples?

_____

7. You have  Can you get two tacos?

_____

8. You have  Can you get two hot dogs?

_____

CREATIVE THINKING ACTIVITY

Can You Guess?

How many of these riddles can you guess? Write your answers on the lines.

1. What opens every day and closes every night, but does not sell anything?

a flower

2. What loses its head every morning but gets it back at night?

3. What is full of holes but can hold a lot of water?

4. What can you put on but never wear?

LANGUAGE ACTIVITY

Picture This

Did you know that you can write messages using pictures? A rebus is a kind of puzzle that uses pictures for words. Can you figure out what each rebus below says? Write the word under each picture.

 +

before

Now write what this rebus says.

 never  a  + pull .

 never hope 2 C I.

But  tell U N +  + how,

 + d  + her C T +  – d B I!

On another piece of paper, try to make your own rebus. Leave spaces between the words. Use a + sign to link sounds that make one word. Give your rebus to a friend to figure out.

49

offoff

off

offoffoffoff

offoffoffoffoffoff

offoffoff

off

offoffoffoffoff

offoffoffoff

offoffoffoffoffoffoffoff

offoffoffoff

offoffoffoffoffoffoffoffoffoffoff

offoffoffoffoffoffoffoffoffoffoffoffoffoffoffoff

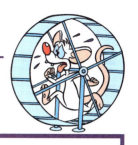
Sand Pouring

3. Open a paper clip all the way. Hold it against the inside of the jar, and push it into all the sand. Pull it out and see how pretty the sand looks. Make these designs all around the jar. You can try other ways of making designs in the sand, too.

4. Spoon sand to the top of the jar and put on the lid. You did it!

SCIENCE ACTIVITY

On Track

Do you know who made these tracks? Match the tracks with the correct animals on the next page. Write the name of the animals on the line.

dog

(continued)

52

SCIENCE ACTIVITY

On Track

dog

turtle

cat

rabbit

deer

sea gull

frog

53

Let It Grow

You can grow your own grass, even if there is snow outside! Follow the directions below for growing grass in a shape.

You Will Need: paper, scissors, a sponge, a pen, some grass seed

1. Pick a shape you want your grass to grow in. Draw it on paper that is the same size as your sponge. You could make a star, a circle, or the first letter of your name!

2. Cut the paper shape out.

3. Trace the shape on the sponge with a pen.

4. Cut the shape out of the sponge.

5. Wet the sponge a little and put grass seed all over the top.

1. Draw **2.** Cut **3.** Trace **4.** Cut **5.** Grow!

Look at it every day. Put more water on it if it feels dry. Soon you will have green grass growing right before your eyes!

ORAL PRESENTATION

What Did You Dream?

Write a paragraph about your favorite dream. Read your paragraph to a friend or family member.

My Favorite Dream

DRAMA ACTIVITY

How Do You Help?

This is an activity for you to do with one or more friends.
Think of all the ways you can help around the house. Act out something you do to help. Let your friends guess what you are doing.

These are some things you can act out:

bake a cake	water the plants	dust the furniture
make your bed	walk the dog	put your things away
mop the floor	wash the dishes	juggle three bowling balls
feed the fish	rake the leaves	wash the windows
change the baby	shovel the snow	give the dog a bath
wash the car	pull up weeds	read a book to the baby

LANGUAGE ACTIVITY

Oday youay eatyay udmay?

Pig Latin

Pig Latin is a funny way you can speak. This is how you speak in Pig Latin:

1. You take a word and move the first consonant or consonant cluster (for example, th) to the end of the word.

2. Next you add "ay" to the end of the word.

3. If the word begins with y, simply add "ay" to the end of the word.

4. If the word begins with a vowel, add "yay" to the end of the word.

For example: **baby=abybay, brush=ushbray, yellow=yelloway, and eat=eatyay** in Pig Latin.

Write these Pig Latin words.

Yesay _____Yes_____   eallyray _____

otDay _____   unnyfay _____

ayssay _____   ingsthay _____

Now write a letter in Pig Latin to a friend. Ask your friend to write back to you!

RESEARCH AND REPORTING ACTIVITY

What's My Name?

You know that a baby beaver is called a kit, a baby elephant is a calf, and a baby lion or bear is a cub. Some animals have different names for the mother and father, too.

The animal names on the left are all mixed up. Can you put them in the right place? Use books to help you.

kid
cow
ewe
duckling
gander
buck
calf
drake
nanny
chick
fawn
sow
gosling
hog
ram
hen

Mother	Father	Baby
goose	gander	
		piglet
	bull	
doe		
	rooster	
		lamb
duck		
	goat	

Crack The Code

There are many different kinds of codes. Crack each coded message below. Read the clues to help you.

1. EKOJ SI YADOT DROWSSAP EHT

   Clue: This message is written backwards.

   The password today is joke.

2. LOO KFO RME INT HEB IGC AGE

   Clue: The spaces between the words are in the wrong place.

   _____

3. ZPVS TFDSFU JT TBGF XJUI NF

   Clue: Change each letter to the one that comes before it in the alphabet.

   _____

4. 3-8-1-14-7-5 20-8-5 3-15-4-5 1-20 14-15-15-14

   Clue: The number *1* stands for *A, 2* stands for *B*, and so on. Write the alphabet under the numbers 1–26.

   _____

Use these codes to write your own secret message to a friend. Then make up your own codes to share.

CREATIVE THINKING ACTIVITY

What's My Name?

Here is a guessing game you can play in a group. The name of the game is "What's My Name?"

One player thinks of a person everyone knows. It can be a real person, or it can be a character from a book, movie, or television show.

Then the player gives a few clues to help the others guess the name. Can you guess the name from the clues below?

I am cute.
I have two brothers.
I wear a flower in my hair.
And I'm cute!

The other players take turns guessing. If no one can guess, the players can ask for another clue. The first player to say the right name gets to be the next mystery person.

CRITICAL THINKING ACTIVITY

NAME _____

What Comes Next?

Look at these number patterns. What number comes next? Write the number in the blank.

1 2 3 1 2 3 1

1 2 2 3 1 2 2 3 1 2

Now figure out the picture patterns below. Draw the picture that comes next in each pattern.

moon   planet   sun   star   comet   asteroid

61

SCIENCE ACTIVITY

Don't Believe Everything You See

Sometimes your own eyes play tricks on you! Look at the pictures below and answer the questions.

Is the hat taller or wider? Really?

_____
- - - - - - - - - - - - - - - -
_____
- - - - - - - - - - - - - - - -
_____

Which line seems longer? *Is* it longer?

_____
- - - - - - - - - - - - - - - -
_____
- - - - - - - - - - - - - - - -
_____

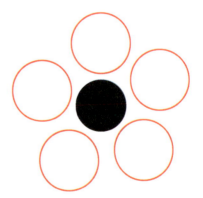

Which dark circle seems bigger? Is it?

_____
- - - - - - - - - - - - - - - -
_____
- - - - - - - - - - - - - - - -
_____

(continued)

Don't Believe Everything You See

Do you see the candle?
What else do you see?

_____
- - - - - - - - - - - - - - - - -
_____
- - - - - - - - - - - - - - - - -
_____
- - - - - - - - - - - - - - - - -
_____

Hole in the Hand

1. Roll a piece of paper into a tube.

2. Close your right eye.

3. Now hold the tube up to your left eye.

4. Look through the tube at something across the room.

5. Put your right hand next to the tube.

6. Now open your right eye. You will see your hand with a hole in it!

63

CREATIVE THINKING ACTIVITY

Pick The Winner!

Choose your favorite story or character. Use words and pictures to make a medal for the winner. Then, on the lines, write why you like the story or character best.

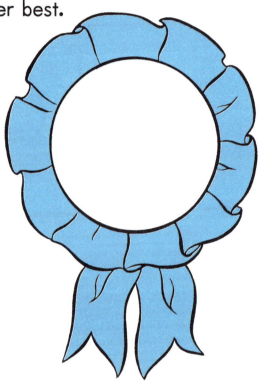

_____

- -

_____

- -

_____

- -

_____

ANSWER KEY

Name

LANGUAGE ACTIVITY

Bingo

Ask some of your friends to play this game with you.

Make a grid similar to the one below for each player.

Players should write each word below in one box of the grid. The words can be in any order.

Have one of your friends read the words in random order, one at a time. The players should circle each word on their paper as the word is said.

The person who circles three words in a row should call out "Bingo!"

Continue playing until all the words have been called out.

jump	likes	to
cage	and	read
go	see	tiny

Answers	will	vary.

3

Name

PROBLEM SOLVING ACTIVITY

Go Home

Use your finger to trace a path through the maze to connect the dog to the puppy. Then use a blue crayon to mark the path. Use a different colored crayon to connect each of the other animals to its friend.

Can you help (Runt) go to the (puppy)?

Can you help (Buttons) go to (Mindy)?

Can you help (Squit) go to the (baby bird)?

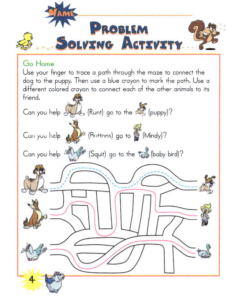

4

Name

ART ACTIVITY

What Can You See?

Think about what you might see in a birdcage, a refrigerator, a fish tank, and out of a window. Draw a picture to illustrate each scene.

Answers will vary.

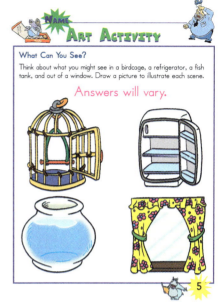

5

Name

SCIENCE ACTIVITY

Where Do I Live?

Look at the animal pictures at the bottom of the page. Draw a line from the animal to the box showing where it lives. Think about other animals that are found in each setting. Circle the animals that could be pets.

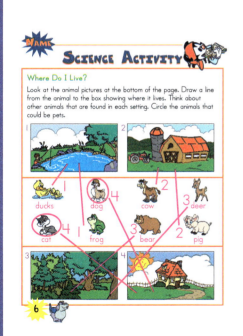

ducks 1   dog 4   cow 2   deer 3

cat 4   frog 1   bear 3   pig 2

6

Name

CRITICAL THINKING ACTIVITY

What Can You Ride?

Here is an activity that you can do with a friend.

Put an X on the things that you can ride on land. Draw a line under the things you can ride on water. Circle the things that you can ride in the air.

On another sheet of paper, draw other things that you can ride.

plane	pigeon	sailboat	car
horse	rocket	bicycle	tree
monkey bars	skateboard	dog	yacht
balloon	moon	submarine	cat

7

Name

MATHEMATICS ACTIVITY

Find the Pets

Find and count the dogs, cats, birds, and fish in the picture. Write the numbers on the lines.

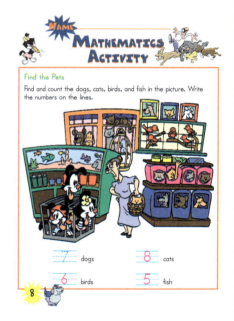

7 dogs   8 cats

6 birds   5 fish

8

65

ANSWER KEY

CRITICAL THINKING ACTIVITY

What Is In It?

Identify each object on the left and decide which object in the row would most logically be inside. Circle your choices.

bag	pumpkin	sandwich	book
box	bat	trophy	doll
flowerpot	tree	grass	flower
ring box	necklace	ring	pen
shoe box	hat	pants	boots
tent	cot	bunk bed	stove

9

ART ACTIVITY

Make a Pet Robot

Here is an activity for you to do with a friend.

You will need to gather the following materials: large and small cereal boxes, craft sticks, pipe cleaners, bottle caps, buttons, beads, paste, and colored markers.

Once you have finished creating your pet robots, tell each other stories about your pets.

10

LANGUAGE ACTIVITY

My Dog

Unscramble the words in each group to make a sentence. The first word in each sentence is in the right place. Write each sentence on the lines.

1. I big dogs like.

   I like big dogs.

2. My is dog big.

   My dog is big.

3. My swim can't dog.

   My dog can't swim.

4. I dog park to the walk my.

   I walk my dog to the park.

11

MATHEMATICS ACTIVITY

Time Out!   Answers will vary.

Look at the sample clock and digital watch at the top of the page. The long hand on the clock shows the minutes and the short hand shows the hour. Show the time when you do each activity on the clock and write the time on the digital watch.

2:00

I get up at this time.

I go to school at this time.

I go out to play at this time.

I eat dinner at this time.

I go to bed at this time.

12

LANGUAGE ACTIVITY

Shape Up!

Put the words listed below in the right shape. Look carefully at the shape of the letters to make sure they fit in the spaces.

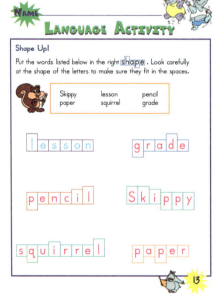

| Skippy | lesson | pencil |
| paper | squirrel | grade |

l e s s o n   g r a d e

p e n c i l   S k i p p y

s q u i r r e l   p a p e r

13

SOCIAL STUDIES ACTIVITY

May I?

Look at the pictures at the bottom of the page. Write the number of each picture next to the sentence that describes it.

You may do this in the water.	6	You may not do this in the water.	4
You may do this at the zoo.	1	You may not do this at the zoo.	3
You may ride like this.	7	You may not ride like this.	5
You may play here.	2	You may not play here.	8

14

66

ANSWER KEY

ART ACTIVITY

Come Out and Play!

Think of a book you like to read. Who do you wish could come out and play with you? Draw a picture.

Answers will vary.

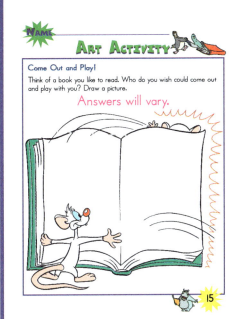

15

SOCIAL STUDIES ACTIVITY

Stop and Go

What color is STOP?   What color is GO?

Look at the first box. Look at the color of the light that is showing, then choose and circle the object in the box that is usually the same color as the light. Repeat this activity with the other boxes.

16

LANGUAGE ACTIVITY

Make A Word

Draw a line from a trailer to the back of each car to complete a word.

Answers may vary.

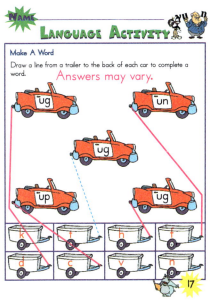

17

SCIENCE ACTIVITY

Sail Away!

You can make a boat!
Ask an adult to do this activity with you.
Find the following materials: an empty half-gallon milk carton, a square of paper, a plastic straw, and a piece of clay.

1. Cut the milk carton in half, or have an adult cut it for you.

2. Color the square of paper and punch three holes in it with a pencil, as shown.

3. Run a straw through the paper and stand the straw in the carton. Hold it in place with a piece of clay.

Set your boat afloat in a pond, pool, or tub.

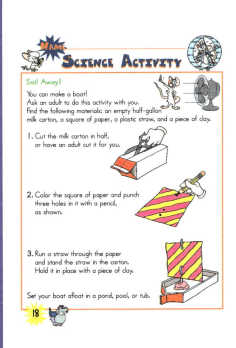

18

LANGUAGE ACTIVITY

Moon Code

Each symbol used below stands for a letter. Use the code. Write the words. Then say the words.

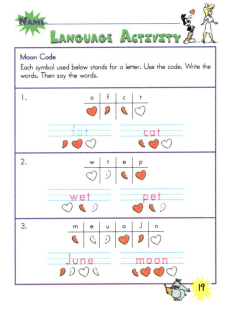

1. a f c t
   fat   cat

2. w t e p
   wet   pet

3. m e u o J n
   June   moon

19

CREATIVE THINKING ACTIVITY

Circle Fun

A circle can be a sun. What else can it be? Draw a picture using each circle.

Answers will vary.

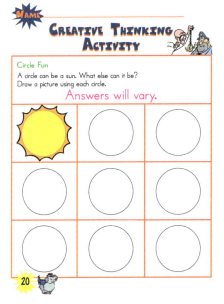

20

67

ANSWER KEY

LANGUAGE ACTIVITY

What Is My Name?

Each letter of the alphabet has a symbol. Use the code to make names. Write the names.

Skippy

Runt

Pesto

Mindy

Write your name in code. _Answers will vary._

21

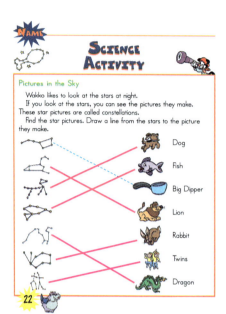

SCIENCE ACTIVITY

Pictures in the Sky

Wakko likes to look at the stars at night.

If you look at the stars, you can see the pictures they make. These star pictures are called constellations.

Find the star pictures. Draw a line from the stars to the picture they make.

Dog
Fish
Big Dipper
Lion
Rabbit
Twins
Dragon

22

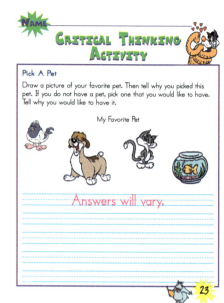

CRITICAL THINKING ACTIVITY

Pick A Pet

Draw a picture of your favorite pet. Then tell why you picked this pet. If you do not have a pet, pick one that you would like to have. Tell why you would like to have it.

My Favorite Pet

Answers will vary.

23

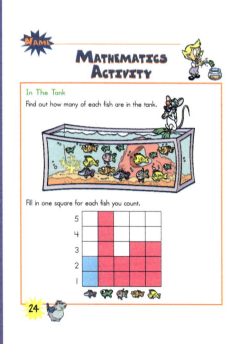

MATHEMATICS ACTIVITY

In The Tank

Find out how many of each fish are in the tank.

Fill in one square for each fish you count.

24

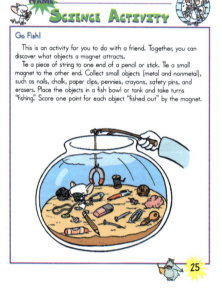

SCIENCE ACTIVITY

Go Fish!

This is an activity for you to do with a friend. Together, you can discover what objects a magnet attracts.

Tie a piece of string to one end of a pencil or stick. Tie a small magnet to the other end. Collect small objects (metal and nonmetal), such as nails, chalk, paper clips, pennies, crayons, safety pins, and erasers. Place the objects in a fish bowl or tank and take turns "fishing." Score one point for each object "fished out" by the magnet.

25

PROBLEM SOLVING ACTIVITY

At The Beach

Read each sentence. Then draw a picture showing the scene described in each sentence. _Placement of answers will vary._

1. Three shells are by the water.

2. Bits of wood are by the water.

3. A bird is in the sky.

4. A fish is jumping out of the water.

5. A little green boat is in the water.

green

26

ANSWER KEY

ART ACTIVITY

Picture Frame Collage

Use shells to make a frame collage. If you can't find shells, use pasta shells! Other materials you will need are a square of cardboard, scissors, paint, glue, and tape.

Read the directions. Frame a photograph of yourself to give as a gift to a member of your family.

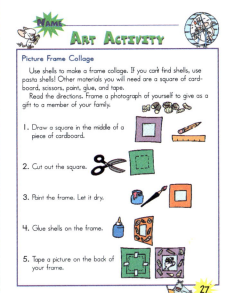

1. Draw a square in the middle of a piece of cardboard.

2. Cut out the square.

3. Paint the frame. Let it dry.

4. Glue shells on the frame.

5. Tape a picture on the back of your frame.

27

DRAMA ACTIVITY

Finger Puppet Play

Do this activity with one or more friends. Make puppets! Put on a play!

Gather old gloves, scissors, markers, bits of felt, and glue. Read the directions.

Practice your parts and present a puppet play to your family and friends.

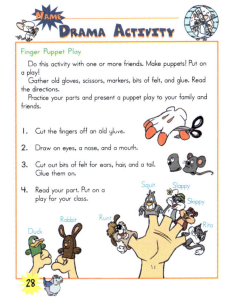

1. Cut the fingers off an old glove.

2. Draw on eyes, a nose, and a mouth.

3. Cut out bits of felt for ears, hair, and a tail. Glue them on.

4. Read your part. Put on a play for your class.

Squit Slappy Skippy Duck Rabbit Runt Rita

28

SOCIAL STUDIES ACTIVITY

Make Up Your Mind!

What do you like to do?
Put a check next to the thing you like to do best.
Sit down with a friend. Find out what your friend likes to do. Find out what things you both like to do.

Answers will vary.

1. Go to the aquarium ___ or go to the zoo ___
2. Swim in the water ___ or walk in the woods ___
3. Look for rocks ___ or look for shells ___
4. Ride on a pony ___ or ride in a boat ___
5. Jump like a frog ___ or hop like a rabbit ___
6. Pet a cat ___ or pet a dog ___
7. Read a book ___ or see a play ___
8. Feed a fish ___ or feed a bird ___
9. Play tag ___ or play ball ___
10. Ride a bus in the city ___ or ride a car in the country ___

29

MUSIC ACTIVITY

Name That Tune!

Yakko likes to sing songs.
What songs do you like to sing?
Write the names of two songs you like.

Answers will vary.

Make a flute to hum your songs. Ask an adult to help you collect a cardboard tube, a pencil, a small square of waxed paper, and a rubber band. Follow the steps listed below to make a flute. Use the flute to hum your songs to a friend. Your friend should try to guess the song.

1. Put four holes in a tube. Use a pencil.

2. Put a piece of waxed paper over one end of the tube.

3. Put a rubber band over the paper to keep it in place.

4. Move your fingers over the holes and hum a song.

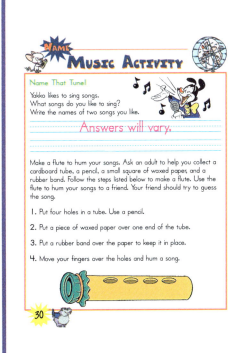

30

ART ACTIVITY

Print A Leaf

Slappy and Skippy like to trace leaves and draw. It is also fun to print leaves.

With a friend, collect the following materials: leaves, glue, cardboard, poster paint, paintbrushes, and drawing paper. Read the directions and follow the steps for making leaf prints.

Try to identify the leaves by looking for them in books.

1. Put glue all around the top of a leaf. The top is the smooth side.

2. Glue the leaf to a piece of cardboard.

3. Put a little paint all over the leaf.

4. Press the cardboard onto a piece of paper. Press hard.

5. Pick up the cardboard. You can print many leaves this way!

31

SOCIAL STUDIES ACTIVITY

New Things

Each year you do many new things. Read each sentence. Write your answer.

Answers will vary.

1. What new thing did you learn to do?

2. What new place did you go to?

3. What new thing did you get?

4. What new book did you read?

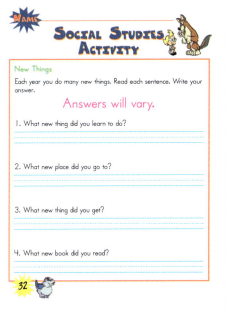

32

69

ANSWER KEY

CREATIVE THINKING ACTIVITY

A Good Name

Elmyra's rabbit looked like a ball of snow. Snowball was a good name for her.

Think of a good name for each animal. Write the name on the line.

On a separate sheet of paper, draw one of the animals you named.

1. A turtle   2. A mouse

  Answers will vary.

3. A cat   4. A lion

5. A frog   6. A pony

33

CRITICAL THINKING ACTIVITY

Did You Hear That?

Read each sentence. Think of when you might say each sentence. Write **winter**, **spring**, **summer**, or **fall** on the lines.

1. "It is fun to play outside in the snow."   *winter*

2. "The red leaves are so pretty."   *fall*

3. "It is too hot to play in the sun."   *summer*

4. "Did you see the new green leaves?"   *spring*

5. "It will be cold soon."   *fall*

34

PROBLEM SOLVING ACTIVITY

Find A Word

Find each of the words in the puzzle and circle them. Words are written vertically and horizontally.

flower	tree	string	wolf	fish	nuts
blast	house	squirrel	hat	spring	gray

```
w  s  q  a  n  p  f  h  b  s
h  n  u  t  s  l  i  a  m  q
u  r  g  h  o  u  s  e  q  u
b  l  g  p  r  l  c  s  n  x  i
a  h  a  t  o  m  p  i  l  r
s  e  v  n  w  r  r  m  g  e
l  t  r  e  e  e  g  i  y  a
i  w  a  t  r  m  n  d  a
n  s  t  r  i  n  g  t  y  n
```

35

RESEARCH AND REPORTING ACTIVITY

Animal Book

Pick an animal to tell about. Make a book about the animal you pick. Look in a book. Try to find out these things.

1. What does it look like?   Answers will vary.

2. Where does it live?

3. How does it move?

4. What does it do during the day?

5. What does it do at night?

6. What does it eat?

7. What can it do that is special?

Write what you find out about your animal. Use as many pages as you need.

Make a cover for your book. Write the name of your animal and draw a picture. Then put all of the pages together.

36

SCIENCE ACTIVITY

Blowing In The Wind

Make a pinwheel and see it turn in the wind!

Gather the following materials: a square of paper, crayons, scissors, a thumbtack, and a pencil with an eraser. Follow the directions below.

1. Take a square piece of paper. Color both sides.

2. Draw two lines and a circle. See the picture.

3. Cut along each line up to the circle.

4. Fold four corners to the middle. See the pictures.

5. Put a thumbtack in the middle to hold all the ends.

6. Put the thumbtack into the eraser end of a pencil.

Now, hold on tight and be careful the wind's not too strong or you could end up flying to Holland.

37

CRITICAL THINKING ACTIVITY

Which Is It?

Your <u>kite</u> ought to be like your <u>face</u>—different from everybody elses. Don't you think? If you make a kite of your own, you could draw a big picture on it so you could see it when your kite was flying. If you and some friends were flying your kites together, you would know which kite was yours.

What about these kites? They all look the same, don't they? One kite is different. Look closely. Find the kite that is different. Then circle the two things that make it different.

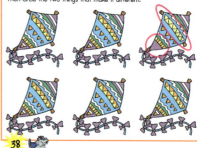

38

70

ANSWER KEY

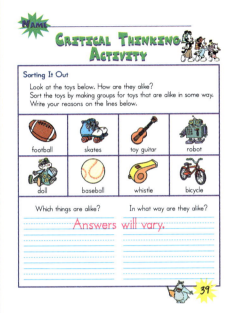

Name

CRITICAL THINKING ACTIVITY

Sorting It Out

Look at the toys below. How are they alike?
Sort the toys by making groups for toys that are alike in some way.
Write your reasons on the lines below.

football	skates	toy guitar	robot
doll	baseball	whistle	bicycle

Which things are alike?	In what way are they alike?
Answers will vary.	

39

Name

LANGUAGE ACTIVITY

Busy Words

Many words mean more than one thing. Read each pair of sentences. Find the word below that can fit in both sentences. Write the word in each blank.

light	play	fly	watch
change	right	leaves	fall

1. a. My dog never does anything ___right___ .

   b. I write with my ___right___ hand.

2. a. There is a ___fly___ in my soup!

   b. The bird learned to ___fly___ .

(continued)

40

Name

LANGUAGE ACTIVITY

Busy Words

3. a. Carlos turned on the ___light___ .

   b. The little dog is very ___light___ .

4. a. The ___leaves___ are on the ground.

   b. I don't like it when my grandmother ___leaves___ .

5. a. Yakko and Dot ___play___ in the park.

   b. Emily saw the ___play___ Snow White.

41

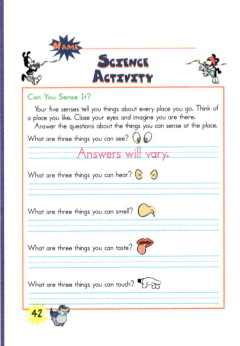

Name

SCIENCE ACTIVITY

Can You Sense It?

Your five senses tell you things about every place you go. Think of a place you like. Close your eyes and imagine you are there.
Answer the questions about the things you can sense at the place.

What are three things you can see?

Answers will vary.

What are three things you can hear?

What are three things you can smell?

What are three things you can taste?

What are three things you can touch?

42

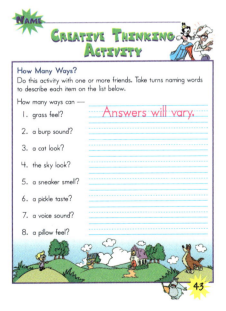

Name

CREATIVE THINKING ACTIVITY

How Many Ways?

Do this activity with one or more friends. Take turns naming words to describe each item on the list below.

How many ways can —

1. grass feel?
2. a burp sound?
3. a cat look?
4. the sky look?
5. a sneaker smell?
6. a pickle taste?
7. a voice sound?
8. a pillow feel?

Answers will vary.

43

Name

LANGUAGE ACTIVITY

Time For A Rhyme

Yakko, Wakko, and Dot were "as snug as three bugs in a rug."
The words *snug, bug,* and *rug* rhyme.
Look at the sentences below. Look at the list of words below and find the one that rhymes with the underlined words in each sentence.
Write a rhyming word in the blank. Be sure the sentence makes sense.

took	word	mat	bed	night

1. The <u>cat sat</u> on the ___mat___ .

2. <u>Look</u> at the <u>book</u> I ___took___ .

3. The Brain has a <u>light</u> to <u>write</u> at ___night___ .

4. I thought I <u>heard</u> that <u>bird</u> say a ___word___ .

5. We <u>fed</u> baby <u>Ned</u> and put him to ___bed___ .

44

71

Answer Key

Science Activity

Shapes To Feel

"Taking over the world requires a good sense of touch. Sometimes I have to touch Pinky sharply on the shoulder to make him think. But your friends are probably smarter.

Make a touching box with one of them. Make sure that you have the following: cardboard, scissors, scraps of velvet, sandpaper, sponge, satin, felt, plastic, corduroy and other materials, glue, and a shoe box.

One of you should read the directions for making the box. Be sure it's you."

1. Cut shapes out of cardboard. Make two of each shape.

2. Now cut shapes to match out of different things. You can use velvet, sandpaper, sponge, satin, felt, or plastic. Glue the shapes on the cardboard.

3. Glue one set of shapes to the top of a shoe box. Cut a hole in one end of the shoe box so that your hand can fit in. Put the other set of shapes in the box.

4. Put your hand in the box and feel one of the shapes. Tell which one you think it is. Then take it out and match it to the shape on the top of the box. If you are right, you get one point. Take turns and match all the shapes.

45

Mathematics Activity

Food For Sale

Write **Yes** or **No**. Then tell how much change you will get or how much more you need.

 FISH 45¢   PIZZA 50¢   HOTDOG 25¢   TACO 30¢

 APPLE 5¢   BANANA 7¢   ICE CREAM 10¢ MILK 6¢

1. You have
   Can you get an ice cream?   Yes, 5¢

2. You have
   Can you get two milks?   No, 4¢

3. You have
   Can you get a fish?   Yes, 15¢

(continued)

46

Mathematics Activity

Food For Sale

4. You have
   Can you get a banana?   Yes, 3¢

5. You have
   Can you get pizza?   No, 5¢

6. You have
   Can you get three apples?   Yes, 2¢

7. You have
   Can you get two tacos?   No, 10¢

8. You have
   Can you get two hot dogs?   Yes, 5¢

47

Creative Thinking Activity

Can You Guess?

How many of these riddles can you guess? Write your answers on the lines.

1. What opens every day and closes every night, but does not sell anything?

   a flower

2. What loses its head every morning but gets it back at night?

   a pillow

3. What is full of holes but can hold a lot of water?

   a sponge

4. What can you put on but never wear?

   a play

48

Language Activity

 Dance

Picture This

Did you know that you can write messages using pictures? A rebus is a kind of puzzle that uses pictures for words. Can you figure out what each rebus below says? Write the word under each picture.

 + 4   +   B + (ring)

before   tiny   bring

Now write what this rebus says.

never ___ a ___ + pull .

never hope 2 C I.

But ___ tell U N + ___ + how,

___ + d ___ + her C T + ___ – d B !!

I never saw a purple cow. I never hope to see one. But I can tell you anyhow, I'd rather see than be one!

On another piece of paper, try to make your own rebus. Leave spaces between the words. Use a + sign to link sounds that make one word. Give your rebus to a friend to figure out.

49

Art Activity

Sand Pouring

"The best place to find sand is by the ocean or in the desert. But it's one color: brown. Brown's dull. You can find aquarium sand in a store. It comes in different colors, which is why fish like it.

Surprise someone you know with a pretty gift you can make yourself.

Gather the following materials: newspaper, colored aquarium sand, a medium-sized jar with a lid, a spoon, and a large paper clip. Read and follow the directions for making a sand-poured jar. And be careful. Sand is a messy business."

1. Put newspaper on the table where you are working.

2. Spoon some sand into the jar, until it looks like a band. Then take another color, and spoon another band of sand into the jar. Keep putting different colors of sand into the jar, until it comes almost to the top.

(continued)

50

72

ANSWER KEY

ART ACTIVITY

Sand Pouring

3. Open a paper clip all the way. Hold it against the inside of the jar, and push it into all the sand. Pull it out and see how pretty the sand looks. Make these designs all around the jar. You can try other ways of making designs in the sand, too.

4. Spoon sand to the top of the jar and put on the lid. You did it!

51

SCIENCE ACTIVITY

On Track

Do you know who made these tracks? Match the tracks with the correct animals on the next page. Write the name of the animals on the line.

dog
cat
rabbit
sea gull
deer
frog
turtle

(continued)

52

SCIENCE ACTIVITY

On Track

dog

turtle

cat

rabbit

deer

sea gull

frog

53

SCIENCE ACTIVITY

Let It Grow

You can grow your own grass, even if there is snow outside! Follow the directions below for growing grass in a shape.

You Will Need: paper, scissors, a sponge, a pen, some grass seed

1. Pick a shape you want your grass to grow in. Draw it on paper that is the same size as your sponge. You could make a star, a circle, or the first letter of your name!
2. Cut the paper shape out.
3. Trace the shape on the sponge with a pen.
4. Cut the shape out of the sponge.
5. Wet the sponge a little and put grass seed all over the top.

1. Draw   2. Cut   3. Trace   4. Cut   5. Grow!

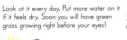

Look at it every day. Put more water on it if it feels dry. Soon you will have green grass growing right before your eyes!

54

ORAL PRESENTATION

What Did You Dream?

Write a paragraph about your favorite dream. Read your paragraph to a friend or family member.

My Favorite Dream

Answers will vary.

55

DRAMA ACTIVITY

How Do You Help?

This is an activity for you to do with one or more friends.
Think of all the ways you can help around the house. Act out something you do to help. Let your friends guess what you are doing.

These are some things you can act out:

bake a cake	water the plants	dust the furniture
make your bed	walk the dog	put your things away
mop the floor	wash the dishes	juggle three bowling balls
feed the fish	rake the leaves	wash the windows
change the baby	shovel the snow	give the dog a bath
wash the car	pull up weeds	read a book to the baby

56

73

Answer Key

Language Activity

Pig Latin

Pig Latin is a funny way you can speak. This is how you speak in Pig Latin:

1. You take a word and move the first consonant or consonant cluster (for example, th) to the end of the word.

2. Next you add "ay" to the end of the word.

3. If the word begins with y, simply add "ay" to the end of the word.

4. If the word begins with a vowel, add "yay" to the end of the word.

For example: **baby**=abybay, **brush**=ushbray, **yellow**=yelloway, and **eat**=eatyay in Pig Latin.

Write these Pig Latin words.

Yesay	**Yes**	eallyray	**really**
otDay	**Dot**	unnyfay	**funny**
ayssay	**says**	ingsthay	**things**

Now write a letter in Pig Latin to a friend. Ask your friend to write back to you!

57

Research and Reporting Activity

What's My Name?

You know that a baby beaver is called a kit, a baby elephant is a calf, and a baby lion or bear is a cub. Some animals have different names for the mother and father, too.

The animal names on the left are all mixed up. Can you put them in the right place? Use books to help you.

kid
cow
ewe
duckling
gander
buck
calf
drake
nanny
chick
fawn
sow
gosling
hog
ram
hen

Mother	Father	Baby
goose	**gander**	**gosling**
sow	**hog**	piglet
cow	bull	**calf**
doe	**buck**	**fawn**
hen	rooster	**chick**
ewe	ram	lamb
duck	**drake**	**duckling**
nanny	goat	**kid**

58

Language Activity

Crack The Code

There are many different kinds of codes. Crack each coded message below. Read the clues to help you.

1. EKOJ SI YADOT DROWSSAP EHT
   Clue: This message is written backwards.
   The password today is joke.

2. LOO KFO RME INT HEB IGC AGE
   Clue: The spaces between the words are in the wrong place.
   Look for me in the big cage.

3. ZPVS TFDSFU JT TBGF XJUI NF
   Clue: Change each letter to the one that comes before it in the alphabet.
   Your secret is safe with me.

4. 3-8-1-14-7-5 20-8-5 3-15-4-5 1-20 14-15-15-14
   Clue: The number *1* stands for A, *2* stands for B, and so on. Write the alphabet under the numbers 1–26.
   Change the code at noon.

Use these codes to write your own secret message to a friend. Then make up your own codes to share.

59

Creative Thinking Activity

What's My Name?

Here is a guessing game you can play in a group. The name of the game is "What's My Name?"

One player thinks of a person everyone knows. It can be a real person, or it can be a character from a book, movie, or television show.

Then the player gives a few clues to help the others guess the name. Can you guess the name from the clues below?

Dot

I am cute.
I have two brothers.
I wear a flower in my hair.
And I'm cute!

The other players take turns guessing. If no one can guess, the players can ask for another clue. The first player to say the right name gets to be the next mystery person.

60

Critical Thinking Activity

What Comes Next?

Look at these number patterns. What number comes next? Write the number in the blank.

1 2 3 1 2 3 1   **2**

1 2 2 3 1 2 2 3 1 2   **2**

Now figure out the picture patterns below. Draw the picture that comes next in each pattern.

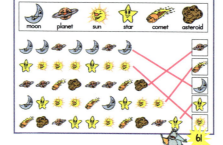

moon   planet   sun   star   comet   asteroid

61

Science Activity

Don't Believe Everything You See

Sometimes your own eyes play tricks on you! Look at the pictures below and answer the questions.

Is the hat taller or wider? Really?

The hat looks taller, but the height and length are the same measure.

Which line seems longer? *Is it longer?*

The vertical line seems longer, but both lines are the same length.

Which dark circle seems bigger? Is it?

The circle on the left seems bigger, but both circles are the same size.

(continued)

62

ANSWER KEY

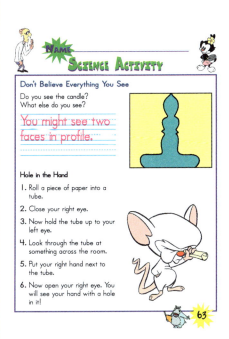

Science Activity

Don't Believe Everything You See

Do you see the candle?
What else do you see?

You might see two
faces in profile.

Hole in the Hand

1. Roll a piece of paper into a tube.
2. Close your right eye.
3. Now hold the tube up to your left eye.
4. Look through the tube at something across the room.
5. Put your right hand next to the tube.
6. Now open your right eye. You will see your hand with a hole in it!

63

Creative Thinking Activity

Pick The Winner!

Choose your favorite story or character. Use words and pictures to make a medal for the winner. Then, on the lines, write why you like the story or character best.

Answers will vary.

64

McGraw-Hill Consumer Products

The skills taught in school are now available at home!
These award-winning software titles meet school guidelines and are based on
The McGraw-Hill Companies classroom software titles.

MATH GRADES 1 & 2

These math programs are a great way to teach and reinforce skills used in everyday situations. Fun, friendly characters need help with their math skills. Everyone's friend, Nubby the stubby pencil, will help kids master the math in the Numbers Quiz show. Foggy McHammer, a carpenter, needs some help building his playhouse so that all the boards will fit together! Julio Bambino's kitchen antics will surely burn his pastries if you don't help him set the clock timer correctly! We can't forget Turbo Tomato, a fruit with a passion for adventure, who needs help calculating his daredevil stunts.

Math Grades 1 & 2 use a tested, proven approach to reinforcing your child's math skills while keeping him or her intrigued with Nubby and his collection of crazy friends.

TITLE
Grade 1: Nubby's Quiz Show
Grade 2: Foggy McHammer's Treehouse

MISSION MASTERS™ MATH AND LANGUAGE ARTS

The Mission Masters™—Pauline, Rakeem, Mia, and T.J.—need your help. The Mission Masters™ are a team of young agents working for the Intelliforce Agency, a high-level cooperative whose goal is to maintain order on our rather unruly planet. From within the agency's top secret Command Control Center, the agency's central computer, M5, has detected a threat...and guess what—you're the agent assigned to the mission!

MISSION MASTERS™ MATH GRADES 3, 4, & 5

This series of exciting activities encourages young mathematicians to challenge themselves and their math skills to overcome the perils of villains and other planetary threats. Skills reinforced include: analyzing and solving real-world problems, estimation, measurements, geometry, whole numbers, fractions, graphs, and patterns.

TITLE
Grade 3: Mission Masters™ Defeat Dirty D!
Grade 4: Mission Masters™ Alien Encounter
Grade 5: Mission Masters™ Meet Mudflat Moe

MISSION MASTERS™ LANGUAGE ARTS GRADES 3, 4, & 5

This series invites children to apply their language skills to defeat unscrupulous characters and to overcome other earthly dangers. Skills reinforced include: language mechanics and usage, punctuation, spelling, vocabulary, reading comprehension, and creative writing.

TITLE
Grade 3: Mission Masters™ Freezing Frenzy
Grade 4: Mission Masters™ Network Nightmare
Grade 5: Mission Masters™ Mummy Mysteries

BASIC SKILLS BUILDER K to 2 – THE MAGIC APPLEHOUSE

At the Magic Applehouse, children discover that Abigail Appleseed runs a deliciously successful business selling apple pies, tarts, and other apple treats. Enthusiasm grows as children join in the fun of helping Abigail run her business. Along the way they'll develop computer and entrepreneurial skills to last a lifetime. They will run their own business – all while they're having bushels of fun!

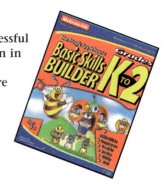

TITLE
Basic Skills Builder –The Magic Applehouse

TEST PREP – SCORING HIGH

This grade-based testing software will help prepare your child for standardized achievement tests given by his or her school. Scoring High specifically targets the skills required for success on the Stanford Achievement Test (SAT) for grades three through eight. Lessons and test questions follow the same format and cover the same content areas as questions appearing on the actual SAT tests. The practice tests are modeled after the SAT test-taking experience with similar directions, number of questions per section, and bubble-sheet answer choices.

Scoring High is a child's first-class ticket to a winning score on standardized achievement tests!

TITLE
Grades 3 to 5: Scoring High Test Prep
Grades 6 to 8: Scoring High Test Prep

SCIENCE

Mastering the principles of both physical and life science has never been so FUN for kids grades six and above as it is while they are exploring McGraw-Hill's edutainment software!

TITLE
Grades 6 & up: Life Science
Grades 8 & up: Physical Science

REFERENCE

The National Museum of Women in the Arts has teamed with McGraw-Hill Consumer Products to bring you this superb collection available for your enjoyment on CD-ROM.

This special collection is a visual diary of 200 women artists from the Renaissance to the present, spanning 500 years of creativity.

You will discover the art of women who excelled in all the great art movements of history. Artists who pushed the boundaries of abstract, genre, landscape, narrative, portrait, and still-life styles; as well as artists forced to push the societal limits placed on women through the ages.

TITLE
Women in the Arts

Visit us on the Internet at:

www.MHkids.com

Or call 800-298-4119 for your local retailer.

Most titles for Windows 3.1™, Windows '95™ & '98™, and Macintosh™.

McGraw-Hill Consumer Products

All our workbooks meet school curriculum guidelines and correspond to
The McGraw-Hill Companies classroom textbooks.

SPECTRUM SERIES

DOLCH Sight Word Activities

The DOLCH Sight Word Activities Workbooks use the classic Dolch list of 220 basic vocabulary words that make up from 50% to 75% of all reading matter that children ordinarily encounter. Since these words are ordinarily recognized on sight, they are called *sight words*. Volume 1 includes 110 sight words. Volume 2 covers the remainder of the list. Over 160 pages.

TITLE	ISBN	PRICE
Grades K-1 Vol. 1	1-57768-429-X	$9.95
Grades K-1 Vol. 2	1-57768-439-7	$9.95

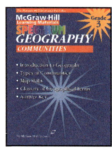

GEOGRAPHY

Full-color, three-part lessons strengthen geography knowledge and map reading skills. Focusing on five geographic themes including location, place, human/environmental interaction, movement, and regions. Over 150 pages. Glossary of geographical terms and answer key included.

TITLE	ISBN	PRICE
Gr 3, Communities	1-57768-153-3	$7.95
Gr 4, Regions	1-57768-154-1	$7.95
Gr 5, USA	1-57768-155-X	$7.95
Gr 6, World	1-57768-156-8	$7.95

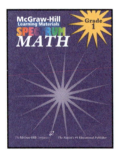

MATH

Features easy-to-follow instructions that give students a clear path to success. This series has comprehensive coverage of the basic skills, helping children to master math fundamentals. Over 150 pages. Answer key included.

TITLE	ISBN	PRICE
Grade 1	1-57768-111-8	$6.95
Grade 2	1-57768-112-6	$6.95
Grade 3	1-57768-113-4	$6.95
Grade 4	1-57768-114-2	$6.95
Grade 5	1-57768-115-0	$6.95
Grade 6	1-57768-116-9	$6.95
Grade 7	1-57768-117-7	$6.95
Grade 8	1-57768-118-5	$6.95

PHONICS

Provides everything children need to build multiple skills in language. Focusing on phonics, structural analysis, and dictionary skills, this series also offers creative ideas for using phonics and word study skills in other language arts. Over 200 pages. Answer key included.

TITLE	ISBN	PRICE
Grade K	1-57768-120-7	$6.95
Grade 1	1-57768-121-5	$6.95
Grade 2	1-57768-122-3	$6.95
Grade 3	1-57768-123-1	$6.95
Grade 4	1-57768-124-X	$6.95
Grade 5	1-57768-125-8	$6.95
Grade 6	1-57768-126-6	$6.95

SPECTRUM SERIES – continued

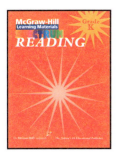

READING

This full-color series creates an enjoyable reading environment, even for below-average readers. Each book contains captivating content, colorful characters, and compelling illustrations, so children are eager to find out what happens next. Over 150 pages. Answer key included.

TITLE	ISBN	PRICE
Grade K	1-57768-130-4	$6.95
Grade 1	1-57768-131-2	$6.95
Grade 2	1-57768-132-0	$6.95
Grade 3	1-57768-133-9	$6.95
Grade 4	1-57768-134-7	$6.95
Grade 5	1-57768-135-5	$6.95
Grade 6	1-57768-136-3	$6.95

SPELLING

This full-color series links spelling to reading and writing and increases skills in words and meanings, consonant and vowel spellings, and proofreading practice. Over 200 pages. Speller dictionary and answer key included.

TITLE	ISBN	PRICE
Grade 1	1-57768-161-4	$7.95
Grade 2	1-57768-162-2	$7.95
Grade 3	1-57768-163-0	$7.95
Grade 4	1-57768-164-9	$7.95
Grade 5	1-57768-165-7	$7.95
Grade 6	1-57768-166-5	$7.95

WRITING

Lessons focus on creative and expository writing using clearly stated objectives and pre-writing exercises. Eight essential reading skills are applied. Activities include main idea, sequence, comparison, detail, fact and opinion, cause and effect, and making a point. Over 130 pages. Answer key included.

TITLE	ISBN	PRICE
Grade 1	1-57768-141-X	$6.95
Grade 2	1-57768-142-8	$6.95
Grade 3	1-57768-143-6	$6.95
Grade 4	1-57768-144-4	$6.95
Grade 5	1-57768-145-2	$6.95
Grade 6	1-57768-146-0	$6.95
Grade 7	1-57768-147-9	$6.95
Grade 8	1-57768-148-7	$6.95

TEST PREP
From the Nation's #1 Testing Company

Prepares children to do their best on current editions of the five major standardized tests. Activities reinforce test-taking skills through examples, tips, practice, and timed exercises. Subjects include reading, math, and language. Over 150 pages. Answer key included.

TITLE	ISBN	PRICE
Grade 1	1-57768-101-0	$8.95
Grade 2	1-57768-102-9	$8.95
Grade 3	1-57768-103-7	$8.95
Grade 4	1-57768-104-5	$8.95
Grade 5	1-57768-105-3	$8.95
Grade 6	1-57768-106-1	$8.95
Grade 7	1-57768-107-X	$8.95
Grade 8	1-57768-108-8	$8.95

Visit us on the Internet at:
www.MHkids.com